MONEY·
·WISE
Meditations

MONEY·
·WISE
Meditations

To Be Found Faithful in God's Audit

JOHN H. RUDY
Foreword by Wally Kroeker

HERALD PRESS
Scottdale, Pennsylvania
Kitchener, Ontario

Library of Congress Cataloging-in-Publication Data
Rudy, John H., 1924-
  Moneywise meditations.

  1. Stewardship, Christian—Meditations.   2. Christian
giving—Meditations.   I. Title.
BV772.R83   1989   241'.68   89-2191
ISBN 0-8361-3486-9 (alk. paper)

The paper used in this publication meets the minimum requirements of
American National Standard for Information Sciences—Permanence of
Paper for Printed Library Materials, ANSI Z39.48-1984.

MONEYWISE MEDITATIONS
Copyright © 1989 by Herald Press, Scottdale, Pa. 15683
    Published simultaneously in Canada by Herald Press,
    Kitchener, Ont. N2G 4M5. All rights reserved.
Library of Congress Catalog Card Number: 89-2191
International Standard Book Number: 0-8361-3486-9
Printed in the United States of America
Illustrated by Mary Chambers
Design by Gwen M. Stamm

95 94 93 92 91 90 89 10 9 8 7 6 5 4 3 2 1

DEDICATION

To Lucy, whose love, understanding, and encouragement have so greatly enriched and facilitated my stewardship ministry during all the years of our life together.

CONTENTS

FOREWORD

"Stop worrying about your money, your gold and silver," the preacher thundered. "You can't take it with you anyway, and even if you could it would only melt."

No doubt a fictitious story, but it illustrates one end of the money debate, that money is wicked and its owners depraved and hell-bound. It's not a viewpoint North American Christians find comforting, for we are an affluent bunch, and if money is beyond redemption we are in big trouble.

But we know enough not to trust the opposite extreme either, the view that wealth is proof of God's blessing and that God wants to make us rich. Most of us know too many godly folk who *aren't* rich to take that view seriously.

A lot of Christian money talk has piled up at either end of the spectrum. "Much of our preaching on money," observes Richard Foster, "has been either to condemn it or praise it but not to help each other relate to it."

That's where John Rudy comes in. He provides the fresh approach Foster is talking about.

For my money, John's approach to the Christian use of mammon makes a lot of sense. He's realistic; money is here to stay and we may as well get used to it. He's also radically biblical: money can be hazardous to your health. Like fire, it's a better servant than master.

Money is more than a means of exchange. It doesn't just sit there in our wallets idling in neutral. It has its own kind of power. And this power can be used for good or evil.

Money is also a mirror of who we are, for as James Moffat has said, the treatment of money—how it is earned and how it is spent—is one of the most decisive tests of a person's character.

As a well-traveled stewardship ambassador for the Mennonite Church, John Rudy is spreading the good news about money—that it does not have to seduce and dominate. It can be very useful for sharing, exercising Christian compassion, correcting inequities, promoting economic justice, building the church, and extending the kingdom of God.

John is both priest and prophet. "I like money," he says affirmingly. He does not disparage those who have wealth (as long as they have earned it honestly and ethically) but rather encourages a wholesome respect for money and its potential influence. Yet there is also the clear voice of the prophet calling us to account. One cannot come away from these writings without being nudged toward more faithful Christian discipleship.

He echoes Clement of Alexandria, the second-century church father who said, "Wealth is at our disposal, an instrument which can be used well or foolishly. How it is used doesn't depend on the instrument, but on the person who is using it. If we use it well, it is a valuable servant—a servant which can do good things for us, and for those who depend on us. If we use it badly, it is an unhelpful servant—a servant which causes us and our friends endless harm."

That was written eighteen hundred years ago. But it is remarkably current, and the problem it addressed endures today. Money is still a hot topic. Books and magazines abound to explain how to earn it, how to save it, how to shelter it, how to make it grow. Money seems to be on everyone's mind. Richard Foster sees it as one of the three most seductive forces today (along with sex and power).

Money has been called the jugular vein of the spiritual life. No wonder Scripture repeatedly warns about it. We've been told that the Bible devotes 3,000 verses to the topic of material wealth, that one of every ten verses in the Synoptic Gospels contains direct teaching on economic issues. The apostle Paul knew what he was talking about when he said the love of money was the root of all evil (1 Timothy 6:10).

Jesus talked a lot about money.

So does John Rudy.

In this volume John cuts a wide swath—what we think of money, how we get it, what we do with it. He talks about business ethics, stewardship, return on investment, responsible living, charitable giving, estate planning, congregational fellowship and counsel, mutual aid. His writing is lively, his foundation biblical, his topspin practical and down-to-earth.

These meditations have been culled from hundreds written over the years. Many appeared in his "Money Matters" column in the *Mennonite Weekly Review.* Others have appeared in his "Auditor's Report" column in *The Marketplace,* published by Mennonite Economic Development Associates. They are brought together in this volume to encourage, challenge, and affirm.

Martin Luther said Christians need three conversions—heart, mind, and purse. This book will help convert your purse.

It's the right book for those who want to resist the wiles of a greed-gilded age, who want to make their money count for God, who want to firmly lodge their business and fiscal lives under the lordship of Christ.

Wally Kroeker
Editor, The Marketplace
Winnipeg, Manitoba

AUTHOR'S PREFACE

I heard someone say there are two things we have not talked about in church: sex and money. Now there's only one. Money.

Worse yet, it has often been fashionable to be negative about money. We seem to enjoy talking about unrighteous mammon, filthy lucre, and the stinking rich. We thunder against the evils of money, and then pass the offering plates.

I feel it is high time we emphasize the good news about money. In this book, I am trying to suggest that money can be an asset and not just a liability. It offers opportunities and not just problems. Money in the hands of Christians can be good stuff—but it's dangerous.

As our brother Milo Kauffman reminded us, money can be a true friend or a vicious enemy. It can be a faithful servant or a cruel master. It can serve man or rule him. Money can be a great blessing or a terrible curse.

My purpose in writing these brief meditations is to both affirm and challenge money-making Christians. Many of us have more wealth than ever before. Our wealth can lure us into self-indulgent living. Or we can use wealth to help further the cause of Christ. Privilege leads to responsibility. In spite of the over-

13

whelming needs of the world, we can make a difference with our money, God's money.

I am indebted to Milo Kauffman, Daniel Kauffman, and Dwight Stoltzfus for their inspiration and encouragement. They have been my stewardship mentors.

It is my hope and prayer that the meditations in this book will help nudge many of us to greater faithfulness.

We need a stewardship revival. Perhaps an unusual time of spiritual renewal will come when we bring our money, and our whole estates, under the rule and reign of God.

John H. Rudy
Lancaster, Pa.

MONEY·
·WISE
Meditations

It is required of stewards
that they be found faithful.
—1 Corinthians 4:2, RSV/KJV

Meditations on

CHRISTIAN
STEWARDSHIP

Handle with Care

We sometimes receive packages in the mail with a bold message: HANDLE WITH CARE. It's probably a gift from someone: a china cup and saucer, a glass figurine, a clock, a doll, a toy.

Isn't Christian stewardship something like this? We receive packages from God. They are gifts from him: strength, ability, time, money, heritage, land, relationships. The gift list goes on and on. And aren't the packages always marked HANDLE WITH CARE?

Throughout the Bible we are told that God is the Great Giver. He gives us the ability to produce wealth. He gives strength to his people. God gives good gifts to those who ask him. He gave his only Son. He meets all of our needs. God richly provides us with everything for our enjoyment.

God says, "Receive these gifts. Accept them with joy and gratitude. Manage them responsibly. Share them generously. Employ them in my enterprise. Use them to accomplish my will and purpose. And always HANDLE WITH CARE."

Maybe we begin our stewardship journeys when we freely proclaim, "I am a gifted person!"

What If Everybody Did?

What kind of church would it be if every member were a faithful steward of all his or her resources? If everybody avoided an extravagant lifestyle? If every Christian brother and sister covenanted with each other to give and receive counsel on personal money matters? If everybody gave generously from their incomes? If everybody included the work of the Lord in their wills?

I know, this is a little too idealistic. It would be like heaven. But, right here on earth, we could be a little more faithful. A little more frugal. A little more generous.

God does not expect perfection. But he does call us to greater faithfulness. Right here where we are. Right in the mainstream of the economic order. With money.

Be a Visual Aid

We often make use of visual aids to enhance and clarify our messages. We use pictures and charts and all kinds of things.

The apostle Paul used visual aids. He even used himself. "Keep on imitating me, my brothers. Pay attention to those who follow the right example we have set for you" (Phillipians 3:17 TEV).

Isn't it kind of daring to offer oneself as a visual aid? Sure it is. But like the apostle Paul, empowered by the Spirit of God, we too can offer ourselves as visual aids.

Some people have difficulty understanding the practical applications of Christian stewardship. Show them by your own example. Some people are bewildered about a responsible lifestyle. Show them. Some people want to be more generous. Show them.

When people aren't reading their Bibles as much as they ought, when they are having difficulty understanding the gospel, when they don't seem to be able to find the way—give them a visual aid: you!

I May Be A Millionaire

I keep getting these big fat envelopes in the mail. The bold print catches my attention: "You may have just won one million dollars." I received two of these sweepstakes in a single day.

Isn't it fun to fantasize about a million dollars? We would buy all the things we have always wanted to buy. We would travel to all the places we have always wanted to go. And, of course, we would be generous. My, how generous we would be to our children and to the church.

Then, when we get hold of ourselves again, we quit fantasizing about a million dollars. We realize that we are responsible, under God, only for what we have. We are called to be faithful stewards.

So, why bellyache because we don't have a million? Why not simply thank God and look for the best ways to manage all he sees fit to credit to our accounts?

The key word, be it little or much, is this: faithfulness!

We Are Tenants

Ownership is part of a businessperson's dream. Don't rent. Own. Own real estate, machinery, inventories, accounts receivable.

The capitalistic system allows private property. By holding deeds, certificates, and other legal instruments we become private owners.

As the legal owners of so many things, it is sometimes difficult for us to acknowledge that God is the real and ultimate Owner of everything. He is the Landlord. We are his tenants. We possess, we occupy, we use, we manage—but we don't own.

The Bible is clear. God created the heavens and earth. He made everything in the heaven and earth. Nothing exists that hasn't originated with God. He gives us ability to produce wealth. He gives us strength, wisdom, knowledge, eternal life—even his only Son.

The Owner puts us in charge. We are his managers. We are responsible for all his gifts to us. That's what we call Christian stewardship.

One day each of us, as tenants, will have to give an account to the Landlord.

As we go to our places of tenancy every morning let us pray, "Lord, help me today to faithfully manage and take good care of your property. You have been so extravagant toward me, even though I don't deserve it. I want to provide you with a good return on your investment. Amen."

Borrowed Capital

Under God we enjoy perfect economic equality. We all own exactly the same amount of stuff: nothing, zero, zilch. Everything we have is only a loan from God.

Now, of course, ownership is part of the North American Dream. Don't rent, own. So, we own houses, stocks, bonds, bank accounts, farms, businesses. We have pieces of paper which prove our legal ownership. And that's alright. But, in the final analysis, we are all debtors. We possess, we occupy, we use, but we never own.

Maybe your and my responsibility is something like the power of attorney I have from my mother. I possess her assets, I manage them, I use them. But I had better employ Mother's assets to meet her needs, to carry out her wishes, to achieve her objectives. I have a solemn responsibility. If I misappropriate any of Mother's money for my own selfish benefit, I am guilty of a criminal and immoral act.

Never out of debt. Always in hock. That's your and my situation. All we can do is thank God for his extravagance toward each of us. We are such gifted people!

Gratitude should always lead to generosity.

I'm a Charity Case

We often pride ourselves in making it on our own. Coming up the hard way. Being independent. Self-sufficient.

In fact, we sometimes even belittle people who are habitual recipients of charity. They rely on the benevolence of others. They always need help. We often call them poor managers.

It's tough to admit that we're all charity cases. It's so humbling.

But I've got to make my own personal confession: I'm a charity case. I am. I'm totally dependent upon a loving, benevolent God. All I am and all I have comes from another. They come from God, often through persons whom he uses. I am in constant need of his help, his resources, his guidance, his people.

Sure, I have resources which I call my own. To support my family. To give to the church. But I haven't accumulated these resources all by myself. I'm a recipient of God's charity. And that makes me a charity case.

Yes, I've had opportunities. I have enjoyed good health. I have worked hard like so many other people. But I'm still a charity case.

Maybe you would like to join me in the refrain: We're charity cases!

Stewardship: Get It to the Bottom Line

Every Christian believes in stewardship. We have preached it and taught it as long as we can remember. We affirm the biblical principles. We extol all the virtues of good stewardship.

But profession is not enough. We must do something about it. Christian stewardship is no good until it becomes practical, until we apply it to the bottom line of our everyday economic decisions.

Stewardship should influence our lifestyles, our spending, our borrowing, our investing, our insuring.

We are good stewards when we give generously, when we share with others, when we keep our wills up-to-date, when we do effective estate planning. The purpose is to continue the work Christ began.

It is not enough just to talk about stewardship. Talk is cheap. One way to prove our Christian stewardship is to demonstrate it in our everyday money matters.

I Picked Up a Penny

There's an advantage in being stoop-shouldered. I find more money walking to work.

Lately, with inflation and everything, I haven't picked up pennies. I have seen pennies, but I have limited my stooping to nickels, dimes, and quarters. Seldom do I find a dollar.

The other day, however, I stopped to pick up a lowly penny. Why? Well, that penny on the sidewalk, even though it wasn't worth much, seemed important. It was symbolic. It reminded me that so often we overlook and squander, here and there, a little bit of life and time and ability and material resources.

If all of life is sacred, then even a penny's worth is important enough to be captured and invested wisely.

Now, I'm not suggesting that God hovers over us and records what we do with every single minute and every little penny. But I do believe that in Christian stewardship we are held accountable for whatever God deposits in our accounts, both the big things and the little things.

Full-time Christian Service

Full-time Christian service has often meant that a person must become a pastor. Or a missionary. Or an employee of a church institution.

Isn't business an appropriate arena for full-time Christian service?

The New Testament makes no provision for compartmentalizing our lives into church and business, sacred and secular, holy and profane, Sunday morning and Monday morning. In Christ, secular business becomes sacred.

As followers of Jesus in business, we are called to live the gospel. To be vehicles of the presence of God. To live the life of Jesus. To be different and extraordinary in the daily grind. To be visual aids of faithfulness. To be living epistles.

In the real world of business we have opportunities to demonstrate justice. To exercise compassion. To be sensitive to need. To live responsible lifestyles. To love our partners and our competitors. To provide goods and services which are beneficial to society.

Business is a great place to be engaged in full-time Christian service!

Self-made Millionaires

I get lots of junk mail. Among the junk the other day was this piece: "Two self-made millionaires describe eleven simple rules that can help anyone grow rich . . . money-making skills that have built the fortunes of most self-made millionaires."

One term caught my eye: "self-made." I asked myself, are there any self-made millionaires? Really? Can anyone ever be self-made?

We sometimes like to pride ourselves in being self-made. We started with nothing. We worked and slaved. We didn't have much formal education. We came up the hard way. Then things began to fall into place. We enjoyed success. And we pretend that we did it all by ourselves.

But wait a minute. Scripture pulls us up short: "Beware lest you say in your heart, 'My power and the might of my hand have gotten me this wealth.' You shall remember the Lord your God, for it is he who gives you power to get wealth" (Deuteronomy 8:17-18, RSV).

It's God! That's a humbling confession we all need to make. We are utterly and totally dependent upon God. He is the source of all strength and wisdom and guidance. Too often we forget God. Even as Christians, we have a tendency to give ourselves too much credit for business success.

The only thing we can bring to God is our need. God supplies all the gifts of creation and gifts of redemption. We aren't the rugged, independent entrepreneurs we like to think we are.

Why should it be necessary to experience failure before we discover our dependence upon God?

Meditations on
CHRISTIAN FAITH

Rich in Things
and Poor in Soul

I attended a memorial service. We sang number 434 in *The Mennonite Hymnal*. Part of verse three grabbed my attention: "Rich in things and poor in soul." That's a destructive combination of wealth and poverty.

Now, few of us are as bad off as Fred. In the cartoon he is shown slumped in an easy chair sipping a drink. His wife says to a friend, "Fred is morally bankrupt, but fortunately, he's in great shape financially."

Maybe your confession is much like mine: I'm richer in things than I was ten or twenty years ago. I've accumulated more stuff. My estate is larger. But am I richer in soul? That's the important question. Am I following Jesus closer than I did ten or twenty years ago? Am I more obedient to the Scriptures? Am I a more loving servant? Is prayer a more important part of my life? Am I more compassionate and generous? Am I freer to share my Christian faith?

We're headed for trouble as Christian businesspersons if what we *have* starts becoming more important than *who* we are. It's time to take inventory when we surround ourselves with an abundance of things but feel kind of empty and destitute inside.

We are poorly equipped to be rich in things unless

we are also rich in soul.

You and I need a great deal of spiritual maturity and moral strength to cope with material success. And failure.

Talk with Your Children

We don't talk enough about money at home. We're too secretive. Sometimes we even shut out our spouses from any discussion of family finances.

Our own children are now grown. But when they come home we still talk about money. We talk about making money and spending it. We talk about buying houses, trading cars, giving, saving, investing, writing wills. Our discussions, even using dollar amounts, seem to come naturally. As parents we are deeply grateful for such open communication.

There are some important occasions to talk about money with our children: (1) When the children are at home and we invite their participation in preparing family budgets. (2) When they accompany us to the store and we seize opportunities to model Christian stewardship. (3) When they receive their allowances and we talk about responsible spending and generous giving. (4) When we are older and we write our wills and plan distribution of our estates.

Too often we exclude money from our family conversations. And then, sometime later, poor communication causes broken relationships.

I have seen far too many family conflicts over money which might have been avoided by greater disclosure and more discussion.

Teaching Children About Money

Money was a popular subject at our house when I was growing up. We talked about it all the time. The table conversation between my father and grandfather was often about interest rates, stock prices, bond markets, farm income, business activity, government fiscal policies. I think some of us were even rocked to sleep with a favorite lullaby, "Buy Low, Sell High."

In good times and in bad times, how are money and stewardship values transmitted to the next generation? I doubt that lecturing helps very much. Our children probably don't listen to our sermons. Maybe they listen to our conversations, when they accompany us on a shopping trip, when they see what we put into the offering plate, when they observe the kind of house we live in, when they watch how much we help other people, when they get money of their own to spend, when we allow them to make mistakes, when they are invited to participate in family budget discussions.

Perhaps we excel as teachers when we model good money management and faithful Christian stewardship for our children, when we offer ourselves as visual aids, when we are helpful examples.

Let me use a personal illustration: I don't remember anything my mother preached about feeding the hungry. But I remember the steady stream of persons she fed at our back door. We lived along U.S. Route 30 during the thirties. It seemed that people stopped for a meal almost every day. We called them tramps. Mother never turned anyone away.

Maybe our money actions and economic behavior speak so loudly our children can't hear what we say.

The Black Spot

An economist gave a talk about recession. He started by displaying a big sheet of white paper. He took a marking pen and made a black spot on the paper. The economist then asked the audience what they saw. Everybody replied, "The black spot." Nobody saw the big sheet of white paper.

When it comes to money, don't we usually see only the black spot? It's even fashionable to thunder against the evils of money. We say money threatens our spiritual lives, it becomes an idol, it plays havoc with our relationship with God, it triggers greed and sel-

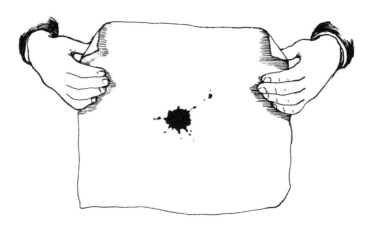

fishness. All of this is true. It's the black spot. But remember, there is still that big sheet of white paper.

We so often overlook the good news about money. Money can be good stuff in the hands of Christians. Good but dangerous. We can use money to help our families, to feed and clothe those in need, to support the work of the church, to extend the kingdom.

My logic, which may be influenced by my training in engineering, leads me to the conclusion that money must be good stuff: (1) Because we pass offering plates in our worship services. (2) Because we give it to our ministers and missionaries. (3) Because our church institutions pay people to collect it. (4) Because our church colleges teach courses in it.

It's high time we take a more positive attitude toward money.

Money Can Be Injurious to Your Health

Money is something like drugs. It can be useful. Or it can be harmful. Money can affect our spiritual fitness.

It all depends on what we do with money. Or what money does to us.

We can use our money for good. To help our families. To feed and clothe those in need. To support the work of the church. To extend the kingdom.

Or we can crave money, stockpile it, misuse its power, squander it on our own selfish indulgences. Then money is injurious to our spiritual health.

Whenever I advocate a positive attitude toward money, whenever I say, "I like money," I must recognize its subtle dangers. Money can abort my Christian faith. It can become an idol. I can become enslaved by it. It can become intoxicating.

You and I need to make sure that our money is not allowed to become injurious to our health.

The Conversion of Tax Collectors

I wish all of us could experience the kind of Christian conversions of two famous revenue agents.

The New Testament records the conversions of two such agents: Matthew and Zacchaeus. They were called tax collectors.

Matthew recorded his own conversion quite simply: "Jesus ... saw a tax collector, named Matthew, sitting in his office. He said to him, 'Follow me.' Matthew got up and followed him" (Matthew 9:9, TEV).

Luke tells us about Zacchaeus: "Jesus went on into Jericho. ... There was a chief tax collector there named Zacchaeus, who was rich. ... Zacchaeus hurried down and welcomed [Jesus] with great joy. ... Zaccheus said ... 'I will give half my belongings to the poor, and if I have cheated anyone, I will pay him back four times as much. ...' Jesus said ... 'Salvation has come to this house today'" (Luke 19:1-10).

These conversions reveal a profound truth: When we decide to follow Jesus our possessions become redirected. Faith affects our finances. There is liberation. Money is set free for the purposes which God intended.

Perhaps Martin Luther was right. He said every Christian needs two conversions: one of the heart and another of the pocketbook.

Foreign Currency

The New Testament tells us we are foreigners, aliens, strangers. Christians are citizens of the colony of heaven.

This truth suggests an interesting thought: The money we make and possess must be "foreign currency." We only do business with this currency as we travel through this foreign land.

Some of us have had the experience of traveling through foreign countries. We exchange our dollars into the currencies of those countries. And we conduct business transactions with those foreign currencies only as long as we are in those countries.

We do not assume long-term possession of foreign currency. We place no abiding confidence in it. We do not become attached to it. We only use it as we're traveling through.

Sometimes we place more value on money than it deserves. We make it too important. We become too preoccupied with it.

But remember this: Money is only a tool. It's a good tool. It can help us support our families. Assist our neighbors. Further the work of the kingdom. Carry out the will and purposes of God. But let us always treat it as "foreign currency."

Be Positive About Money

Why are some people so negative about money? They seem to enjoy talking about the evils of money. They cherish feelings of guilt. And they try to impose guilt on their Christian brothers and sisters.

Some even misquote Scripture. They say that money is the root of all evil. That's not true. It is "the *love* of money [which] is the root of all evil" (1 Timothy 6:10, KJV).

The gospel record makes no mention of Jesus ever condemning anyone for making and having money. He was, however, greatly distressed about people becoming enslaved to money, or attached to it. He said money can become a god. He pointed out how the power of money can be abused.

So, money is not evil or sinful. No. But it's dangerous.

Money, in the hands of a follower of Jesus, is a great tool. It provides great opportunities. To help our families. To help others in need. To further the work of the church. To spread the good news.

Money is useful stuff. Accept it. Be grateful for it. And be sure to put it to good use.

Private Property

One of the characteristics of capitalism is private property. We own assets privately: houses, bank accounts, businesses, securities, retirement plans.

The New Testament reports that some of the early Christians sold their private property and made the proceeds available to those who were in need.

Some Christians today raise interesting questions about ownership: Can a person retain private ownership of anything and still be a faithful follower of Jesus? Wouldn't collective or communal ownership make it easier for Christians to be less selfish and less covetous? And more compassionate and more generous?

I have an opinion: We can be faithful followers of Jesus in any economic system. And this includes capitalism, with its provisions for private property. It would not be any easier to be a Christian in any other economic system.

We hold legal title to property. That's called "private ownership." But we acknowledge God's sovereign ownership. He is the sole and absolute Owner. We have only a life lease. We are responsible for faithful management and use of "private property."

What Would You Do with a Million Dollars?

This is a multiple-choice question. You have three choices: (1) Spend it. (2) Invest it. (3) Give it.

It wouldn't be hard to spend the million dollars. Consume it. Buy more things. A fancier house. Longer trips. Greater luxury. Higher on the hog. And why not? Now you can afford it.

Your second choice: Invest the million dollars. You could put it into land, stocks, gold, money-market certificates, a business. You would have substantially more income, and perhaps some capital gains. To spend. To give to your children. To contribute to the church. And then to distribute what's left by way of your will.

You have a third option: Give it. Pray for grace to let go of much of the million dollars. Now. For the work of the Lord. As an outright gift. Or a gift with lifetime income, by way of an annuity or trust.

It's fun to dream about a million dollars, to speculate on what we would do with that much money. We can easily convince ourselves about how terribly generous we would be with a million. We'd give it all away!

But a million dollars isn't a relevant problem for most of us. The important question is simply this: What am I doing with what I do have? That's my

responsibility. To be a good steward. To be as helpful as I can be.

In that great day will each of us be found faithful?

Putting Money Where
Our Morals Are

It's interesting, even unbelievable, how we Christians sometimes fail to put our money where our mouths are. Our practices sometimes lag our public declarations.

For example, we can pray for peace and invest in war. Or we can abhor alcoholism and put our savings into companies which produce alcoholic beverages. Or we can work for social betterment and let our retirement money go into businesses which are socially irresponsible.

We should be applying investment guidelines which promote world peace, contribute toward social betterment, avoid objectionable industries, insist on responsible management.

What in the world is your money doing? Where in the world is your money going? How in the world is your money helping?

Both our money and our lives should be invested in ways which further the purposes of God.

How we invest our money must be in harmony with what we say we believe.

Money Talks

Our money may be talking so loudly people can't hear what we say. Think about it. Our money may be shouting our loudest testimonies.

Now, of course, money has no voice of its own. By itself, it has no ability to say anything. It can't give its own witness. But money is a kind of public-address system. It amplifies and broadcasts our faith and our beliefs.

That's a startling thing about money. It's silent until we do something with it. Then it talks. It says something about our priorities. It articulates our theology. It discloses our commitment. It reveals our values.

We can talk until we are blue in the face. We can preach with vigor. We can respond at every testimony meeting. We can use the biblical vocabulary. But maybe, as someone has said, the real story of our Christian dedication is told on the stubs of our old checkbooks. Our money talks.

Money is one of faith's indicators. It's an index and a window to the soul. It's a sounding trumpet. It's so vocal that it helps nudge us toward confession and repentance. Thank God for money!

Think what our money could be saying to the world!

God Loves Rich People

It's fashionable to declare that God loves poor people. Sure God loves poor people. But that's not the whole truth. There's also good news for those of us who live in North America: God loves rich people!

"For God so loved the world . . . " (John 3:16). Concerning the rich young ruler: "Then Jesus beholding him loved him" (Mark 10:21, KJV).

What an encouragement this is! Even we are never beyond the reach of God's love and concern.

Why should we suffer under a load of guilt? Why should we become distressed if God has allowed us to accumulate wealth through no faults of our own? Why not admit that the system has been good to us, and then go on?

We are blessed with unprecedented opportunity: To use our possessions for the benefit of those in need. To extend the kingdom of God.

One does not need to baptize wealth. There's a better way: Liberate it. Let God redeem it. Put it to good use.

I Still Like Money!

I've been going around the church making a reckless confession: I like money!

It's interesting to watch the reactions of people. Some smile. Some frown. Some relax. Some look startled. Some raise their eyebrows. But none of my brothers and sisters has ever really challenged my confession. So I still like money!

Now, of course, I hope I don't *love* money, because that would be "the root of all evil." I hope I am not obsessed with money. Enslaved by it. Preoccupied. Intoxicated.

Sure, money is dangerous. I know that. But it can also be extremely useful. It allows us to seize opportunities for good. To help our children. To share with others. To extend the kingdom. To demonstrate our faithful Christian stewardship.

Maybe it's high time we quit scolding each other about money and take a more positive attitude toward it.

Four-letter Words

We usually abhor four-letter words. They're often filthy. Obscene. Evil.

But there are some really good four-letter words. They ought to be in all of our vocabularies.

Rich. Many of us have much more than our forebears, more than multitudes around the world. That spells privilege. And privilege means responsibility.

Love. We can love people and show compassion by the use of our money and possessions.

Help. We don't selfishly hoard our material resources. We put them to good use. To help others who are in need.

Give. We look for opportunities to share, to let go for the benefit of others. Our example is Jesus.

Will. Sure we try to take care of our families. But we also include the work of the Lord in our final dispositions.

Bank Vault or
Heavenly Treasure?

I am not opposed to a bank vault. It's a good place to keep valuable documents: deeds, stock certificates, bonds, certificates of deposit. But a bank vault can't possibly hold heavenly treasure.

Remember the words of Jesus, "Do not lay up for yourselves treasures on earth, where moth and rust consume and where thieves break in and steal, but lay up for yourselves treasures in heaven, where neither moth nor rust consumes and where thieves do not break in and steal. For where your treasure is, there will your heart be also" (Matthew 6:19-21, RSV).

What is heavenly treasure? How can Christians send something ahead for their bank accounts in heaven? I can only give you my personal opinion. I think we lay up heavenly treasure by being servants here on earth. By helping others. By sharing the good news. By ministering to the poor. By giving generously.

Those things in your bank vault can be used to lay up heavenly treasure.

Denying Our Wealth

A friend of mine once said, "John, things are really rough. I just bought another house."

I suspect it's sometimes fashionable to talk about tough times. Maybe we're in a cash squeeze, or we moan about prices, or we complain about taxes. We feel compelled to give the impression we're poor. Seldom do we openly rejoice about being greatly blessed. Our acting and pretending make us a little dishonest.

Perhaps the best thing we can do is freely acknowledge our wealth. Then we can thank God and pray for guidance to be more faithful stewards.

The question usually arises, Who's rich? Many of us don't feel rich. We have ways of proving we aren't rich. But as we compare ourselves with past generations, and as we observe multitudes around the world, the answer is clear. We're rich. Most North American Mennonites are rich.

Wealth presents a joyful opportunity. Wealth can be a tool which God allows us to possess and to manage: to express love, to show compassion, to relieve need, to spread the gospel, to help our children, and to further the mission of the church.

Let's try to be more honest. Instead of denying our wealth, let's acknowledge it. And let's use the wealth—God's wealth—to accomplish his will and purposes.

Meditations on
CHRISTIAN LIFESTYLE

Return on Investment

As businesspersons we often measure our performances by using the rate of return on investment. We examine our earnings as a percent of our total assets. Or we use an investment base of equity plus long-term debt.

Now, I hope I am not too irreverent, but I like to think of God as a capitalist (small c). He has invested so heavily in you and me. He made us. He sent his Son to save us. His Spirit lives within us. God equips us. We are part of his endowment fund. And I believe he expects to get a good return on his investment.

At the judgment day, when God audits my performance, I wonder how he will measure return on investment. Will it be by the way I have treated my partners and employees? By my loving service? By the amount of integrity which has gotten to the bottom line? By the accuracy of my expense accounts? By the honesty with which I have prepared my tax returns? By the methods I have used to collect overdue accounts? By my personal lifestyle? By the ways I have used power?

Maybe you and I ought to begin each day with a prayer something like this: "O Lord, I am your investment fund. You are my investment Manager. Help me today to produce a good yield on all the assets you have credited to my account. May you be pleased with the rate of return on your investment in me. Forgive me when my short-term performance is a big zero, or worse yet, a horrible deficit. Don't purge me from your portfolio, but lift me up to higher ground. Amen."

Profiting or Profiteering?

Why do Christians go into business? The reason is usually the same for Christians who go into teaching or nursing or farming. It's simply this: to try to make a living, to make money. And, of course, we aim to satisfy the legitimate needs of people.

The apostle Paul certainly was not opposed to making money by worthy means: "Warn the idle ... mind your own business ... earn your own living ... help the poor ... work hard ... do not be lazy."

So, as Christians we're in business to make money. Why? So we can buy groceries, purchase a car, provide shelter, pay for education and, of course, help others.

Making money in business is described by one word: profit. That's not a dirty word. It simply identifies the gain we hope to realize by selling a product or service for more than it costs. Without gain we can't be in business very long, just as a teacher or nurse can't work for free very long.

If, then, profits are appropriate for Christians in business, just as salaries are appropriate for teachers and nurses, when does profiting become profiteering? In other words, at what point do profits become unreasonable, excessive, obscene, evil? When are we guilty of gouging?

Profit margins, as we all know, come in many sizes.

They vary from one business to another. They fluctuate according to economic conditions and management abilities. They are often controlled by the marketplace. If a businessperson has a good thing going, the free enterprise system soon invites competition and price cutting.

But, if and when the market allows pricing freedom, when does profiting move across the threshold to profiteering? Is it when we extract inordinate gain which causes hardship for a customer? Is it when we charge all the market will bear? Is it when we allow opportunity to excite greed? Is it when we are driven by insatiable, self-indulgent appetites? Is it when fairness is superseded by injustice? Each of us will need to decide.

Let's allow our pricing policies to be governed by Christian conscience before the marketplace imposes its restraints.

Our Loudest Testimonies

Where do you and I give our loudest testimonies? At church? In testimony meetings? In Sunday school classes? In church schools? Where the biblical vocabulary is accepted and appreciated?

Wouldn't it be startling to discover that we might be giving our loudest testimonies by the way we manage our businesses and the way we behave in our professions?

Back home I sometimes accompanied my grandfather to the local farmers' market. He did some of the weekly shopping for my mother. I got the impression that the more pious the farmer looked, the more his behavior behind the market stall had to be watched.

I grew up with the opinion that too many Christians gave their worst testimonies in their business dealings.

Maybe you and I can make our Christian testimonies more authentic and more inviting by being sure we are compensating our employees adequately. By being fair to our suppliers. By being completely open and honest with our bankers. By always providing products and services which are beneficial to society. By charging prices which produce reasonable profits. By avoiding unfair labor practices. By treating our competitors properly. By adopting modest lifestyles. By giving generously.

You and I know that it isn't just a matter of saying the right things at the right time. Or believing the right things. Or serving on church committees. Or attending the services regularly.

Our toughest assignment is to be Christlike right where we are, in our business, in our professions, day in and day out. How very much we need the help of God's Spirit and the support of our Christian brothers and sisters.

Let's make sure that our business and professional behavior faithfully reflects the life and spirit of Jesus. Then more people may want to become part of his community.

The growth of the church may depend upon the quality of our everyday business and professional lives.

Believing and Behaving

I heard about two businessmen who were long on testimony but short on behavior. Business was tough. They finally landed a job painting a church. When they started to run out of paint, they used lots of thinner. No one would notice. Their bill was returned by the pastor, with this note: "Repaint ye and thin no more."

One of my favorite authors, A. W. Tozer, had a message for businesspersons: "The supreme purpose of the Christian religion is to make men like God, in order that they may act like God. True religion leads to moral action. The only true Christian is the practicing Christian."*

Many of us are fluent in biblical language. We learned it from little on up. We can talk quite easily about salvation, faith, prayer, separation, love, peace, idolatry, lust, greed. But how can we demonstrate Christian belief in business behavior? That's the hard question. That's where all of us confess our desperate need for the guidance of God's Spirit and for the counsel of God's people.

The main purpose of the gospel, as we all know, is not simply to provide us with a holy vocabulary. It's

---

* *Of God and Man* (Camp Hill, Pa.: Christian Publications, Inc., 1960), p. 58.

not just religious talk. The gospel must be lived. Right where we are. In our business. In our relationships with partners and employees. In our dealings with customers. In the midst of competition. Smack in the middle of the real world.

You and I are God's gift to the business world. We have received God's Spirit. And, by God's grace we have the potential to become more and more like God—in business.

Chronic Extravagance

You and I don't need any unusual smarts to know that there are times to save money and there are times to spend it. But we need wisdom and divine guidance to know when to save and when to spend.

Some of us are compulsive savers. We hoard money. We don't do very much that costs money. We don't go out much. We just hang on to our money. And we declare saving to be good stewardship.

Others among us may be compulsive spenders. As long as we have any money at all, we never quit spending. We're on a fast track to nonstop acquisition. More is better.

Could it be that both extremes are wrong? If we are bent on always saving we may miss opportunities to celebrate, when a little selective extravagance may be required. But if we are lunging headlong into massive, wall-to-wall extravagance, then such self-indulgence is wasteful and offers little opportunity to carry out our Christian responsibilities to others.

Neither saving nor spending should become an addiction.

The alternative to chronic extravagance is selective extravagance, which allows us to freely spend our savings in responsible ways on those special occasions.

Lord, keep us from letting "selective extravagance" become a license for careless and irresponsible spending.

Is Financial Success Determining Our Lifestyles?

A strange thing happens among us when our businesses prosper, or real-estate values increase, or the stock market booms, or the boss gives us a raise, or we receive an inheritance. We let all of this pave the way to the good life. Now we can afford to consume and build and travel.

Isn't financial success a poor reason for an extravagant lifestyle?

Too often our lifestyles are determined not by the Scriptures. Not by our heritage. Not by the needs of the world. Not by congregational discernment guided by the Holy Spirit. No, too often we simply live at the levels we can afford.

It's amazing how much we borrow from the world around us: Greed. Individualism. Self-indulgence. Pride. Obsession with things. We give the impression, like our neighbors, that we are more concerned about the quantity of life than the quality of life.

Could it be that our standards of living are hindering the growth and prosperity of the church?

Isn't God calling us to enjoy things without becoming intoxicated with them? To live comfortably without indulging in luxury? To be satisfied with what we have without an insatiable craving for more? To pattern our lives after Jesus without thinking we must live like everybody else? To share with others without tenaciously hanging onto possessions for our own selfish benefit?

There is, however, great cause for rejoicing. Many of our brothers and sisters are living responsible lifestyles. They are moderating their consumption. They are controlling their spending. They are living on less than they can afford. They are sharing generously.

I have often wondered what would be most important to me if my doctor told me I had only a year to live.

Getting and Giving

"You've got to get before you can give." Whoever uttered this statement wasn't all that profound. Of course we have to make money before we have any money to give.

Several years ago I served on a churchwide task force. We studied Mennonite attitudes and practices concerning money and other economic matters. We met for hours and hours and wrote pages and pages. Then one day it occurred to me that we could distill everything into two major concerns: (1) How we get it. (2) What we do with it.

Sometimes we become preoccupied with "what we do with it" before we address "how we get it." We may extol tithing and proportionate giving before we examine how we compensate our employees. We can make large contributions without determing if we might be overcharging for our products and services. Institutions declare us major donors when our businesses may be contributing something harmful to society.

Many of us have heard the old story about the bishop who was offered tobacco money. The potential donor assumed the bishop wouldn't accept tainted money for the work of the church. But the bishop surprised the donor by declaring, "Give the money to me. The devil had it long enough."

My point is this: What was this donor's purpose? No doubt there were mixed motives. You and I should not try to redeem and sanctify ill-gotten profits by making generous charitable gifts.

Nonconformity in Business

I grew up with a strong emphasis on nonconformity. In our Mennonite congregation there were standards of how we should look and how we should behave. People were sometimes excommunicated for conforming too much to the world.

But I can't remember anyone being excommunicated for conforming to the world in business practices. I have no memory of nonconformity being applied to business. We were, however, concerned about the "unequal yoke with unbelievers."

As more of us move in the business world, isn't the biblical doctrine of nonconformity more important than ever?

Romans 12:2 might be an appropriate golden text for Christian businesspersons: "Be not conformed to this world, but be ye transformed by the renewing of your mind" (KJV).

How can you and I apply biblical nonconformity to our businesses? It isn't easy, but here are a few suggestions: By making sure all of our products and services are beneficial to society. By loving our neighbors (partners, employees, competitors) as ourselves. By charging prices which produce no more than reasonable profits. By refusing to use the same deceptive advertising our competitors use. By being open and honest with our creditors. By sharing generously with those in need. By avoiding the conventional businessperson's lifestyle and adopting a more responsible standard of living.

We live in a business world where crime and injustice are prevalent. Many are guilty of fraud, dishonesty, greed, pollution, tax evasion. You and I, however, as Christian businesspersons, are called to nonconformity. More specifically, we're called to nonconformity to the norms and values of our society. And we are called to conformity to Jesus Christ.

I like to borrow a lesson from Wall Street. Investors who are skeptical of the way all the big financial institutions are investing money will proceed in the opposite direction. These investors are called "disciples of contrary opinion."

As followers of Jesus in the business world, let us be disciples of contrary opinion. We are headed in another direction. We are part of a counterculture. As Christians we have often called this kind of life "nonconformity." It's still a good biblical doctrine. We must keep updating its application.

What Is Contentment?

Our congregation back home would call for Scripture verses. I often recited one of my boyhood favorites: "For I have learned, in whatsoever state I am, therewith to be content" (Philippians 4:11, KJV).

A lot of years have passed and I'm still trying to discover the meaning of this verse. What is contentment? What does it mean to say that I'm satisfied with my lot in life? How could the apostle Paul sit in jail, with martyrdom down the road, and say he was content? How can we be satisfied with our economic situations and at the same time be dissatisfied with our spiritual maturity?

So many people are trying so hard to make us discontented. Advertisements suggest we can't be content without a more expensive house, a newer car, a longer vacation, a bigger investment portfolio, an expanding business, a fancier wardrobe.

I still have lots of questions about contentment, but I'm sure about one thing: My contentment should not be based on the size of my paycheck or the size of my estate. It has nothing to do with the size of my house or the size of my car. I know I can't buy contentment at a department store or a travel agency. Real contentment is not related to my outward circumstances.

Contentment comes from an inner sufficiency, a

relationship to a Person, a security in Jesus Christ, a life in the community of God's people.

Do you tend to be a little restless and dissatisfied? Do you bellyache because you don't have more? There's a remedy: Draw a little closer to Jesus. Get a better perspective on the fleeting economic achievements of this world. Observe the multitudes who have so much less than you. And then experience the tranquillity of contentment.

Many Shapes and Sizes

I'm convinced that Christian faithfulness comes in many shapes and sizes. There's one body, one spirit, one Lord, one faith. But many shapes and sizes.

For example, I think it would be kind of dull and monotonous if we all adopted the same lifestyle. We would all live in the same size house, drive the same size car, maintain the same size bank account, go on the same size trip. That kind of uniformity could be miserable.

But our many shapes and sizes must be influenced and nurtured by some common biblical admonitions: We are all called to be faithful stewards. We are to avoid selfish extravagance. We are to use our resources for the benefit of others. We are to follow Jesus. We are to extend God's kingdom.

I would not want some kind of legalism to push us all into the same mold. There is something refreshing and invigorating about a variety of shapes and sizes, when all of us in one Christian community are committed to the one Lord.

Go Ahead, You Can Afford It

When a prosperous business provides you with increased income, why not go ahead and spend it? Now you can afford it.

But as Christian businesspersons, is it ever right to let our lifestyles be determined only by what we can afford? What about intentionally limiting our standards of living by living on less than we can afford so resources are available for others?

There are three levels at which we can establish our lifestyles:

1. *What we can afford.* Our incomes can be the sole determinants of our standards of living. Our consumption can increase in direct proportion to our incomes. We can live right up to the limit of our resources. We can work for more so we can live higher.

2. *More than we can afford.* We can buy now and hope to pay later. We can use credit to increase our consumption. We can live beyond our means. We can display the usual marks of affluence without being worth very much.

3. *Less than we can afford.* We can make some deliberate decisions to consume less so we can give more. We can liberate some resources for others. We can live beneath what we can afford. Our standards of living don't have to increase in direct proportion to

our increased income and wealth.

It is my opinion that you and I ought to take some additional steps toward option 3. Why? So we can be more helpful to others. So the work of the church can prosper. So our lifestyles do not become obstacles to Christian fellowship.

So you can afford it. Great. But that doesn't mean you should spend it on your own selfish indulgences.

Baptize Your Worldly Possessions

I have often repeated this story about a baptismal service. As the minister and the applicant went into the stream, the applicant suddenly remembered that he still had his wallet in his pocket. He grabbed for his wallet, to throw it onto the bank. The minister stopped him, "You bring your wallet right with you. That needs to be baptized, too."

What would happen, I have often asked, if all of us would bring our wallets to be baptized. We'd bring all of our real estate, our bank accounts, our stocks, our retirement funds, our business interests.

What if we'd dedicate to God all of our possessions? We'd bring all we have under the rule and reign of God.

That would be revival!

Looking Richer Than We Are

Some people possess a lot but they don't own very much. They enjoy all that creditors are willing to provide.

Our economic system offers us an amazing ability to live beyond our means. We can buy more than we can afford. Our acquisitive yearnings drive us to supplement our incomes with lots of credit.

So, it's really quite easy to have a lot of things without being worth very much. People see our factories, our offices, our houses, our cars, our clothes, our vacations. And they're fooled. They think we're quite rich.

But, as Christians, as followers of Jesus, why would we want to put on such a display? What motivates us to make a big splash? Why pretend to be something we aren't?

Allow me to offer this admonition: Work hard, thank God for whatever income he allows you to receive, exercise extreme caution in the use of consumer credit, adopt a responsible standard of living, spend less than you can afford, and save for legitimate personal and family needs. Then you will have enough to help others and to support the work of the Lord.

Going First Class

There's a popular doctrine afloat in Christian circles: Believe God and be successful. Accept Christ and enjoy prosperity. He intends that people go first class.

I read about someone who preaches "the gospel of happiness now. You can have it all now. If you are poor, you're irresponsible. Prosperity is your divine right."

Now, of course, there are many faithful Christians among us who are enjoying business success. They have worked hard, they have been highly motivated, they have seized opportunities, they have operated in a growing economy—and something happened. They prospered.

Why have they prospered? Does God reward faithfulness with material prosperity? Or is material prosperity incidental to faithfulness?

First, it is important to acknowledge that wealth comes from God. "Remember the Lord your God, for it is he who gives you the ability to produce wealth" (Deuteronomy 8:18, NIV).

Second, we observe many faithful Christians, in fact, multitudes, who are poor. Some are very poor. They're first-class Christians who are not going first class.

You and I are called, first of all, to be faithful followers of Jesus. If God sees fit to allow us to accumulate material possessions, fine. We will thank God, and we will manage and share the resources according to God's will and purposes. But if material success is not in God's plan for us, we will still rejoice and continue to pursue faithfulness.

Driving a Hard Bargain

"Mennonites give their worst testimonies in their business dealings." That's something I heard people say when I was growing up back home. This sad commentary was usually offered when a brother or a sister in our congregation appeared to be too shrewd.

I won't "walk a mile for a Camel," but I will travel fairly long distances for a good bargain. I like bargains. My Pennsylvanina Dutch heritage taught me to enjoy bargains. I'm turned on whenever the ad says "50% off." This worries me sometimes. Why should I feel so good when I pay less than the usual price? Why do I like to brag about how little I paid for something?

Now, of course, you and I must be careful shoppers. In business we usually don't enjoy fat profit margins. So our costs and our selling prices must be subjected to tight control. We must ride herd on inventories and receivables. We can't survive without adequate profits.

But when does a business transaction become a "hard bargain"? I'm not sure when you and I cross that fine line. But maybe it's when we dicker and haggle too long, when we are insensitive to the circumstances of the other person, when we try too hard to wring the last nickel out of a deal, when we argue and connive in the interests of "good stewardship," when we boast about our negotiation prowess, when we take advantage of someone who is over a barrel, when we don't allow the other party to realize a reasonable profit.

If you and I are bargaining so hard that we distract people from the Jesus way, then there's only one word to describe our behavior. Sin.

But Who Will Weigh the Coal?

I enjoy telling the story about two brothers who were in the coal business. Revival meetings came to town. One of the brothers accepted Christ. For weeks he tried to persuade his brother to become a Christian too. One day the unsaved brother responded, "It's fine

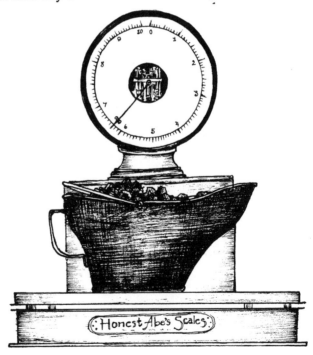

for you to be a Christian, but if I became a Christian, who would weigh the coal?"

Who would weigh the coal! The implication is quite clear. Becoming a follower of Jesus affects how we weigh coal.

When Zacchaeus met the Lord he started to "weigh coal" differently. Luke 19:8 (NIV) records his new business ethics: "Look, Lord! Here and now I give half of my possessions to the poor, and if I have cheated anybody out of anything, I will pay back four times the amount."

If the world's methods for "weighing coal" are off the mark, where do we turn for direction? To the inner nudgings of God's Spirit. To the Scriptures as we study them. To our congregational gatherings as we listen to the admonitions of our brothers and sisters.

"Weighing coal" in today's business world is a complicated enterprise. Pursuing Christian faithfulness is a lifelong journey which requires continuous openness to the leading of God's Spirit plus lots of courage to apply his teachings in our daily business decisions and practices.

How to Survive Wealth

Wealth impoverishes far too many Christians. Our stories often go something like this: The business prospers. We have more money to spend. We begin traveling in different circles. And years later we make the horrible discovery that the price of success has been more than we can afford: broken relationships, family disharmony, loneliness, doubt, alienation from our Christian brothers and sisters.

But the good news is this: Many of our Christian businesspersons are surviving wealth quite well. How are they doing it? There are no ten easy steps, but I think the survivors can be described as follows:

1. They acknowledge God as the source of all wealth. They believe Deuteronomy 8:18 (NIV), "Remember the Lord your God, for it is he who gives you the ability to produce wealth." These survivors aren't ashamed to identify themselves as charity cases. They know they have always been beneficiaries of divine welfare.

2. They scrutinize the business practices they use to accumulate wealth. They seem to be grappling with the right questions: What is a reasonable profit? What is fair compensation for my employees? How should I treat customers who don't pay? Do my products and services contribute something beneficial to society?

What is justice? How can I keep from becoming enslaved by my business?

3. They seek a personal lifestyle which seems responsible. They are, of course, always tempted to go first class. Many of their business associates live high on the hog. But Christian survivors live at a level beneath what they can afford. They seize opportunities to use wealth for purposes beyond their own selfish indulgences.

4. They are generous in their giving and sharing. They set limits on the size of their personal estates. They help their children. They share with needy persons. They liberate significant amounts for various church causes. Survivors seem to realize that they need to give more than the church needs to receive. They work hard at de-accumulation.

5. They participate in the life and mission of the church. They don't allow themselves to become alienated from their congregations. They accept assignments where their abilities can be utilized. They give and receive counsel. They work and pray for the growth and prosperity of the church. Survivors are in the vanguard of Christian faithfulness.

We live in a world which has never seen so much wealth. It's so easy to be well-heeled and dried up. May you and I be numbered among the survivors.

Business Autopsies

What if you and I had all our business affairs opened and examined at death and reported in the daily newspaper? What if all the readers could see our income statements, our balance sheets, our corporate minutes? How would our Christian faithfulness be diagnosed?

Would such business autopsies reveal to our fellow church members that we died in good spiritual health? That we tried to carry out our Christian responsibilities?

Would the autopsies show that we paid adequate wages and benefits? That we charged fair prices? That our business practices were in harmony with what we said we believed? That we handled conflict with love and compassion? That we gave generously?

I don't care if they open my body to discover the cause of death. But what would my brothers and sisters discover if they could see the inside of my business?

What would a business autopsy reveal about you?

The Unequal Yoke

All my life I've heard this Scripture verse recited: "Be ye not unequally yoked together with unbelievers" (2 Corinthians 6:14, KJV). What is an "unequal yoke" in today's climate of business involvements?

I grew up in a family business. We had a salesman named Norm. I remember him as irreverent, foulmouthed, and sometimes half-drunk. Was that an unequal yoke?

J. C. Wenger, in his book *Separated unto God*, suggests that the unequal yoke "involves refusing any business relationship ... which would involve the Christian in any intimate spiritual fellowship with those who are not one with him in faith."*

When the apostle Paul gave his command about the unequal yoke, he was probably referring to a passage in Deuteronomy. Harnessing an ox and an ass to a plow was forbidden. Clean and unclean beasts were not to be hitched together. Paul seemed to use this figurative language to teach the Christians at Corinth. He asked, "What does a believer have in common with an unbeliever?" (2 Corinthians 6:15, TEV).

Many of us were raised on the doctrine of separa-

Separated unto God (Scottdale, Pa.: Herald Press, 1951), p. 87.

tion. We've heard a lot about the church and the world, Christian and non-Christian, the kingdom of light and the kingdom of darkness, the saved and the unsaved. "Come out from among them, and be ye separate, saith the Lord" (2 Corinthians 6:17, KJV).

Now, how does all this apply to today's business relationships? Does it mean that we should not enter into any business partnerships with persons who are not committed to Christian principles? Does it mean that we should not hire unchristian managers? Does it mean that we should acquire no company which has a "corporate culture" which is in conflict with our own Christian mission? Does it mean that we should engage no attorney who would use unethical methods to represent us? Does it mean that we should take on no distributor who would use dishonest devices to sell our products?

I'm not sure. I certainly don't have all the answers. But it seems to me we avoid the unequal yoke when we enter business relationships which help us maintain our Christian integrity, when the relationship helps clarify our Christian identity, when the relationship accentuates our Christian testimony, and when the relationship enhances our expression of Christian love and justice.

Meditations on

CHARITABLE AND PERSONAL GIVING

Size Is Not the Issue

"Bigger is better." "Small is beautiful." Don't we attach too much moral value to size? Why should it matter whether your or my income is little or much, whether our business is small or large, whether our net worths are meager or substantial? Why do we get so hung up on numbers?

If size isn't the issue, then what is? Faithfulness! But how does Christian faithfulness relate to size? By wearing our wealth without being conspicuous. By avoiding gaudy display. By openly confessing God's ownership. By adopting servanthood postures. By dedicating possessions to the needs of others. By employing resources in God's enterprise.

Big or little, large or small, it doesn't make much difference. We all have the same responsibility: To receive gratefully. To manage faithfully. To share generously.

Don't feel guilty if God sees fit to allow you to accumulate a large estate. And don't become jealous if God leads you into opportunities which are not financially rewarding. Just pray for guidance to be faithful, where you are, with what you have.

We will all have to give an account to God, regardless of size.

Quiet Donors

Should you and I as Christians give just to get our pictures in the paper? Or to memorialize ourselves on a plaque? Or to be appointed to a board of directors? Or even to have our names inscribed on a building? Of course not!

We give, like the Macedonians of the apostle Paul's day, because God's grace is at work within us. We give to relieve need. We give to participate in the work of the Lord. We give to help extend his kingdom. We give to demonstrate our love for others. Sometimes we even give to save taxes.

But do we give to make a big fuss, to make a big splash, to make a big impression? No, I don't think that's an appropriate posture for Christian servants.

The admonition of Jesus in Matthew 6 seems pretty clear: "When you give something to a needy person, do not make a big show of it.... When you help a needy person, do it in such a way that even your closest friend will not know about it, but it will be a private matter" (Matthew 6:2-4, TEV).

Giving: Retail or Wholesale?

All of us do "retail giving." Throughout our lifetimes we make numerous gifts from our current incomes. We regularly put something into the offering plate at church on Sunday mornings. We often send checks to our church institutions. Hopefully, we adopt the "firstfruits tithe as a minimum standard for proportionate giving."

But what about "wholesale giving"? Such giving, by way of our will, involves a one-time distribution from our estates. Church causes get the "firstfruits tithe" of our accumulations. Or the charitable bequest is equal to the share each child receives. Or maybe the bequest for the Lord's work is even more "wholesale": Half, or the entire estate in the case of single persons, childless couples, or parents who have wealthy children.

Some of our estates include appreciated real estate and growing business interests—wealth which has never been subjected to the standards of New Testament giving. Our wills become appropriate vehicles for "the crowning act of Christian stewardship."

May our charitable giving be both retail and wholesale.

Don't Just Give Money

I heard an advertisement which went like this: "We need what money can't buy. We need you."

That's a call to voluntarism ... even for businesspersons. The church and the world need more than our money.

Sure, we ought to be giving generously of our money. Maybe we ought to be transferring some things into gift annuities and charitable remainder trusts, which provide lifetime income. Certainly we ought to be including church causes in our wills. But that isn't enough.

We must give ourselves. Our time. Our abilities. Our energies.

Christian businesspeople ought to be volunteers. In our congregations. In our communities. Around the world.

You and I can't get off the hook just by giving our money. Money will not meet all of our Christian responsibilities. We must give ourselves in generous and loving voluntary service.

Embezzlement

When we think of embezzlement we picture a bookkeeper or manager running off with huge sums of the company's money. Embezzlement is stealing or misappropriating something which has been entrusted to us.

Doesn't embezzlement also involve giving leftovers? Giving less than the tithe? Designating nothing in our wills for church causes?

"Will man rob God? Yet you are robbing me. But you say, 'How are we robbing thee?' In your tithes and offerings" (Malachi 3:8, RSV).

God has been so extravagant and lavish toward us. He has entrusted us with so much: life, ability, time, heritage, possessions. Are we being faithful trustees of all God has credited to our accounts?

Maybe we embezzle God's resources when we live selfishly. When we neglect those who suffer. When our proportionate giving is less than the tithe. When we include nothing in our wills for the ongoing work of the church. When we see our brothers and sisters in need and close our hearts against them (1 John 3:17).

There's good news about embezzlement! It's not the unpardonable sin. It can be confessed, forgiven, forsaken. And we can go on to lives of service and generosity. The opposite of embezzlement is faithful stewardship.

Look Before You Let Go

Those fund-raising claims may be exaggerated. The statements may be misleading. The photographs may be deceptive. The story may be overly emotional.

Charitable giving is big business. And it is sometimes a big racket.

How can you keep from being sucked in by slick promotion? How can you tell which charitable organizations are worthy of your support?

Here are some guidelines: The organization's programs should appear consistent with a clear statement of purpose. The purposes and programs of the organization should be in harmony with your Christian beliefs and your understanding of biblical principles. The organization should have a board which is an active and responsible governing body. The organization should make available upon request a comprehensive annual report. You should get prompt responses to your questions. No more than a reasonable amount of your contributions, perhaps less than 30 percent, should go into general administration and fund-raising expenses.

A word of caution seems appropriate: Some charitable organizations are unworthy of your contributions.

Try to be a good steward of your gift funds. Stick with organizations you know and trust. And participate in those programs which help you extend your Christian witness and service.

Someone has said, "Give with your heart—and with your head." That sounds like good advice.

I Dropped the Offering Plate

It was terribly embarrassing. Humiliating. I tried to pass the offering plate with my hand in a cast. And something awful happened.

The wooden plate hit the hard floor. There was money everywhere. I felt everybody was gawking at me. The brotherly and sisterly treatment after the service was not unexpected. "John, we thought you knew how to hang on to money."

It's awful to drop an offering plate. But there's something still worse: To simply pass the plate and to hang on to your money. Or to put in only leftovers.

The prophet Malachi cried out against leftovers. After he reminded the people of God about his extravagance toward them, he told them they were offering to God the leftovers, the lame animals, the runts. He reminded them that even the "Internal Revenue Service" was not content with leftovers.

I don't wish my embarrassment on anyone. It's terrible to drop an offering plate. But it's worse to pass the plate and to hang on to your money, or to put in leftovers.

Double-digit Giving

We're all familiar with double-digit inflation, double-digit interest rates, and double-digit taxes. These are recent developments in North America. We hardly know how to cope with double digits.

But double digits aren't anything new. The Old Testament prescribed double digits. These double digits were called "the tithe." God's people were asked to give 10 percent of their income to the work of the Lord.

The New Testament doesn't seem to demand double-digit giving. But the admonition is more profound: "Every Sunday each of you must put aside some money, in proportion to what he has earned" (1 Corinthians 16:2, TEV).

The Macedonians offer us a good example: "They were extremely generous in their giving, even though they were very poor ... They gave as much as they could, and even more than they could" (2 Corinthians 8:2-3, TEV).

If the Old Testament standard is double-digit giving, is the New Testament standard expressed only in single digits? I don't think so.

Shouldn't we make sure that our giving to the work of the Lord is always expressed in double digits?

Unhappy Tithers

We are too afraid to teach and encourage tithing. We are afraid of being legalistic. We are uncertain about the teachings of the New Testament on tithing.

I serve on a stewardship task force. Our group has talked a lot about tithing. We made a startling discovery: None of us has ever met an unhappy tither! We know only happy tithers.

It was our unanimous opinion that tithing seems to be good for people. It seems to enhance spiritual well-being. It brings joy, fulfillment, satisfaction.

Someone has said, "The tithe is a teacher of stewardship."

Since no one on our task force wants to deprive brothers and sisters of spiritual blessings, it seems good to us that every Christian should be called to adopt the firstfruits tithe as a minimum standard of proportionate giving.

Could it be that Christians need to give more than the church needs to receive?

Pain in the Pocketbook

"Reach out and touch someone's pocketbook." Everybody is adapting the phone company's message to peddle their wares.

Everywhere we turn someone is reaching out and touching our pocketbooks. The supermarket. The automobile dealer. The real-estate agent. The bank. The insurance company. The tax collector. The travel agent. Everybody is telling us what we ought to do with our money.

And then there's the church. Why is it that we get particularly touchy whenever the church reaches out and touches our pocketbooks? Then the nerve to the pocketbook becomes especially sensitive. We experience considerable pain when the church urges us to tithe at least, or even to give until it hurts. We discover we have a low pain threshold.

When it comes to sacrificial giving to the work of the Lord, maybe it's high living that causes the low pain threshold. Or maybe it's high spending. Or high aspirations.

Giving becomes less painful—and even more enjoyable—as we lower our own standards of living and as we demand less for our own selfish indulgences.

The Sacrifice of Leftovers

I'm a little troubled. We may be too much like the people of Malachi's day.

The prophet Malachi reminded his people how much God loved them and how lavishly he had provided for them. But the people responded by sacrificing runts and lame animals—all the leftovers (Malachi 1).

We've been greatly blessed in North America. We enjoy the abundant life. We possess abundant resources. We have abundant opportunities.

But we also have abundant "needs." We complain about high food costs, high interest rates, high housing prices, high educational expenses. But maybe it's high living that creates many of our "needs."

The problem as I see it is this: After we have bought everything we want, and enjoyed everything we want, and gone everywhere we want, we gladly sacrifice the leftovers to the Lord and the work of his church.

God's Word is clear on this matter: He asks for firstfruits rather than leftovers.

You Can Make a Difference

We're sometimes overwhelmed. The needs of the world are so immense. And our resources are so limited.

Sometimes we even suffer feelings of futility and inferiority. It's like trying to outjump a seven-foot basketball player or tackle a 220-pound fullback. It's useless even to try.

When we see so much hunger and so much poverty and so much hopelessness, we're inclined to covet a million dollars. What we would do with a million! How generous we would be!

Since most of us won't ever have a million, the real question comes down to this: What are we doing with what we have?

You and I aren't going to feed the world, or clothe the world, or save the world. But you and I had better be doing what one person can do!

Sure, we have limited resources. But that doesn't lessen our responsibilities. We are called to faithfully manage and generously share whatever God sees fit to credit to our accounts.

You and I, under God, can make a difference!

I Lost My Luggage

It happens every now and then. I fly somewhere to talk about Christian stewardship and disposition of possessions. When I get there I make a beeline for the baggage claim area. No baggage.

Unfortunately, it gives me an illustration for my talk at church that evening. I'm traveling light. I've made disposition of my possessions. But my illustration isn't entirely appropriate. By not getting my baggage I made involuntary disposition of my possession. I am in the congregation to talk about *voluntary* disposition.

We engage in voluntary disposition by what we give during life and by planning the distribution which is to take place after death. By way of lifetime gifts and by way of our wills. To our families. To others in need. To the work of the church.

When I get to heaven I don't expect to find a baggage claim area. I will be traveling light. I'll have no deeds, no stock certificates, no bank accounts, no business interests. Only treasures in heaven.

That's right. I'll make that last great flight without any baggage. I need to plan effective disposition before I go. Now!

"We brought nothing into this world, and it is certain we can carry nothing out" (I Timothy 6:7, KJV).

Meditations on
WILLS AND
ESTATE PLANNING

Do Good Stewards Live Longer?

I have a theory about good stewards. It's probably just a supposition. My supposition is this: That Christians who are faithful managers of their accumulated possessions live longer.

Now, of course, I can't document this. I have no hard data. I have no figures to prove this. But for many years I have made some interesting observations.

A strange tranquillity seems to settle over people after they get their financial houses in order. And the converse also seems to be true: An untidy financial house can be a source of anxiety.

People seem to relax—and maybe live a little longer—when they get their wills up-to-date, when they make provisions for their families, when they let go for the Lord's work.

If I were a doctor perhaps I could relate these financial matters to psychosomatic illnesses. Maybe feelings of guilt from not having a will affects one's health. Maybe it's turmoil over legal complexities, worry about taxes, fear of inadequate retirement income.

But I don't have to be a doctor to notice the joy, the satisfaction, and the fulfillment—even the excitement—when people quit procrastinating. When they complete their estate planning. When they start getting secure income from a gift annuity. When they are relieved of management burdens by way of a charitable remainder trust. When they minimize their tax liabilities. When they participate in the mission of the church.

I don't want to be misunderstood. I am not talking about life after death. Sure, there is eternal life for Christians. Sure, possessions can be used to extend our usefulness long after our work on earth is done.

No, I am suggesting that as good stewards we may live longer, right here and now, if we get our affairs in order. If we plan carefully for the needs of our families and for the work of the church.

Then we can relax and enjoy fulfillment. And live!

Grave Reminders

I walk through Mellinger's Cemetery on my way to work. I can even see names on the tombstones from my office window: Groff, Landis, Lefever, Hoover, Good, Martin.

I wonder how many of these faithful souls died in good financial health. Did they depart with their houses in order?

I don't think I'm a morbid person. But maybe I need these "grave reminders." I look out my window across the cemetery and ask myself, Is my will up to date? Have I provided for my family as best I can? Is a generous portion of my estate designated for the ongoing work of the Lord? Do my children know where all of our important documents are located? When should I give one of our children a power of attorney in case I become incompetent?

These "grave reminders" tell us that life is short. They help spur us to good financial planning, so we can enjoy more time in joyous Christian living.

All Work, No Planning

Many of us businesspeople have contracted the work ethic. It's contagious. We caught a good case from our parents and grandparents.

Work is important. It's good. The Bible tells us to be industrious. There are harsh words for those who are lazy.

But it's so easy to become a workaholic. We can slave away a whole lifetime and accumulate lots of things. But then we devote such little time to planning effective distribution.

I heard a lawyer say we spend 80,000 hours of our lifetimes accumulating possessions and only six hours planning the disposition.

In the parable of the rich farmer, God asked, "Then who will get all these things you have kept for yourself?" (Luke 12:20, TEV). How are you and I answering this important question?

Who will get our things? Will they go to our children? To others? To church institutions? To other charitable organizations?

Planning creative distribution of our possessions, through our wills and lifetime gifts, can be an exciting part of our Christian stewardship.

How Much to Our Children?

We are greatly influenced by tradition, especially when it comes to our estates. Too often we simply give everything to our children, without deciding what they need and how much will be helpful. Sometimes too much money becomes destructive. Sometimes it's a curse rather than a blessing.

I am not suggesting that we disinherit our own children. Of course not. We have a divine responsibility to help them any way we can: when they're growing up, when they go to college, when they buy a house, when they go into business or farming.

But what do our children need when we die, when our wills become effective, when they are already fifty or sixty years old? What about the overwhelming needs of all the other children of the world?

When I talk with parents about their estate planning, they often tell me how well their children are doing. Sometimes the children are making more money than the parents. My response is usually this: Great! I'm happy to hear how successful your children are. Now, what about all the other children: those who are hungry, those who haven't heard the good news, those who lack educational opportunities, those who are suffering hardships?

We can help meet the needs of these other children

by including various church institutions in our wills. We may want to designate the same share each of our own children get. Or maybe we should designate half of our estates, or even more. It depends upon the size of our estates and the legitimate needs of our own children.

Let's use wealth in ways which enrich others rather than in ways which impoverish our own children.

How Much Is Too Much?

Ben Franklin had a saying about people who gave away all their money and then didn't die. He said they were like people who got undressed and didn't go to bed.

Many people are the other extreme. They're afraid to give anything away. They think their large estates may not be enough to meet their needs during the remainder of their earthly stay.

Isn't the way of Christian faithfulness somewhere between these two extremes? On the one hand, it seems imprudent to give everything away and then become dependent upon our families or government. On the other hand, too many of us keep accumulating for all the terrible things which never happen; we don't know when to start de-accumulating.

I have no magic number which signals the point at which we have too much. Christian faithfulness comes in many different sizes. But perhaps we are accumulating too much when we allow our personal wealth to go beyond reasonable expectations of need, beyond legitimate amounts for retirement living, health care, inflation, etc. Excessive and indiscriminate accumulation could be hazardous to our spiritual welfare.

My counsel, particularly to older people, is often this: Be generous with yourself. Keep what you think you will need. Give as much as you can to your children and to church causes. Maintain an estate which is well within your worry level. Then, by the way of your will, make sure your things will go where you want them to go. You won't need them Over There.

Why Not Liberate Your Money

We spend most of our lives bringing money into captivity. Working hard. Accumulating things. Corralling possessions. Earning. Keeping. Conserving. Even hoarding.

What about this kind of slavery? We know it's immoral and unchristian to enslave people. Might it also be wrong to enslave material possessions?

Actually, there is no way we can keep our money captive forever. It will eventually be liberated. Turned loose. If our money isn't emancipated during our lifetimes, it will certainly gain its freedom at our deaths.

Maybe we are both captors and liberators, as we attempt to follow Jesus in our economic system. We corral possessions and then set them free. For the needs of others. For the work of the kingdom.

Where's your money? All tied up? Liberation could bring you peace, joy, fulfillment.

Even your government encourages you to liberate your money. By offering tax incentives.

Sure, you need to be concerned about letting go of your money too soon. But there is also the danger of hanging on too long.

Liberate your money. By way of your will. Or in lifetime gifts. According to God's will. To your children. To others in need. To the work of the church.

Hanging On and Letting Go

We are such acquisitive creatures. And we usually try to hang on to all we are able to acquire.

More money, more land, more product lines, more stocks, more business interests. We spend our whole lifetimes accumulating.

But there comes a time when hanging on is no longer possible. At death we are forced to let go.

Letting go requires some careful planning. Your first obligation is to your family. You try to meet their legitimate needs. But beyond that you have responsibilities to the ongoing work of the Lord.

As a minimum, you may want to tithe your estate, with a tenth to church causes. Or maybe you should "adopt the Lord" as one of your children, with equal shares to church causes and to the children. For some people the charitable bequest should be much larger.

Letting go, carefully and joyfully, is in the true spirit of Christian stewardship. You do this by giving generously during life and by maintaining an up-to-date will.

Are You Still Procrastinating?

I heard someone say he'd like to procrastinate, but he never seems to get around to it.

Procrastination, particularly when it comes to your will, is too costly. You can't afford it. Loved ones may be neglected. Taxes may be higher. The church won't receive anything. Your Christian stewardship will be incomplete.

Actually, procrastination is reckless, because it means your possessions will be distributed according to the government's formula. And procrastination is dangerous, because sometime it is going to be too late to write a will of your own.

Decide how you want your possessions distributed and how you want your loved ones cared for. Decide how much should go to the work of the Lord. Then reach for a phone and make an appointment with your lawyer.

When is the best time to make a will or to bring your present will up-to-date? Right now!

Intestacy Is not a Physical Disorder

Intestacy has nothing at all to do with an abdominal affliction. It's not a medical term.

Intestacy is a legal problem. It concerns the laws which regulate the distribution of your possessions when you die without a will.

Actually, intestacy is a moral ailment. It's a stewardship disorder. It describes Christian irresponsibility.

The one way to treat the infirmities of intestacy is to make a will of your own: For the specific needs of your family. For the work of the kingdom. To minimize taxes. To achieve your Christian objectives.

You don't have to succumb to the grave problems of intestacy. It's curable. The prescription is simple: Make a will. And keep it up-to-date.

Christians who make wills and get their financial houses in order may even live a little longer.

Where Is Your Lard Can?

My grandfather kept good records. When he died we found everything neatly bundled and arranged in a lard can.

Lard cans may no longer do the job. There are now better places to keep important documents and information.

Be sure to let people know where your things are located. Even a will is no good unless it can be found.

Every now and then my wife and I update a couple of sheets of paper which contain important details: the location of our safe-deposit box, our wills, bank accounts, deeds, stock certificates, tax returns, retirement plan, insurance policies. We outline some funeral instructions. We then sign and date these papers and give copies to our children.

At your death it should not be necessary for your survivors to go on a hide-and-seek venture to find your things.

Hearses and U-hauls

"Who says you can't take it with you?" That's the question my friend Mose Slabaugh in Virginia once asked. He pictured a hearse pulling a U-haul trailer.

Now, of course, both Mose and I are familiar with the apostle Paul's words in 1 Timothy 6:7, "We brought nothing into this world, and it is certain we can carry nothing out" (KJV).

It's no secret that both Mose and I came into this world with nothing. No clothes. No bank accounts. No deeds. No stock certificates. No business interests.

And that's exactly the way we'll leave. With nothing. No baggage at all. We're only in charge of a few things for a while.

Maybe the only thing we can do is to make some deposits in our heavenly accounts now. Jesus told us to "lay up treasures in heaven." Maybe we do this by using our money and our time and all of our resources to help people. To share with those in need. To communicate and live God's message. To be the serving presence of Jesus wherever we find ourselves. To dedicate ourselves to the will and purposes of God.

Don't depend on the hearse and the U-haul. Take time now to plan the effective use and distribution of your possessions.

Meditations on
CONGREGATIONAL LIFE

The Good Life in Bad Times

What's happening to the "good life"? For many, it seems to be slithering down the drain.

We may have high hopes for the economy: Thriving companies. Better jobs. More money. Bigger houses. Newer cars. Increasing real-estate values. Larger estates. Even more happiness.

But then something happens and it all seems to be in jeopardy. It's scary. In no time we can be thrust into a new situation of high interest rates, high unemployment, high fuel prices, increasing business failures, plunging real-estate values.

Maybe we've been lulled into thinking that the "good life" is somehow related to things. That it has something to do with our incomes, our net worths, our affluence, our prospering businesses.

How can we cope? How can we make our payrolls? How can we keep the farm? How can we save the business?

It's easy to be glib about all this. Talk is kind of cheap. But through the pain and distress of bad times, we may be able to discover what is really the "good life." We may be able to get new perspectives on material things. We may be able to discover how much we need our Christian brothers and sisters. We may be able to wean ourselves away from depending on so much credit. We may have to adopt more responsible standards of living. We may be able to turn more of our attentions to the needs of others who are so much worse off. We may be able to enjoy more Christian fellowship in our congregations.

None of us covets bad times. None of us enjoys a recession, or reduced income, or declining real-estate values, or loss of a job, or a business that fails. But could it be that God wants to use bad times to lead us to a fresh discovery of the "good life"?

Hindered Fellowship

One of my deep concerns for Christian business-people is this: Too often we allow ourselves to become alienated from our congregations.

I know how critical some of our own non-business brothers and sisters can be. We're suspect when we succeed. And we're suspect when we fail. It seems like a no-win situation.

Right in our own congregations, of all places, we are sometimes made to feel like villains. People accuse us of being unethical, unjust, greedy. They say we're too individualistic, too insensitive, too whatever.

My counsel is this: Let's listen to the admonition of our brothers and sisters. Let's determine, by God's grace, to be in the vanguard of faithfulness. Let's lead the way into more obedient discipleship. And, by all means, let's continue to commit ourselves to loving service right in the midst of the congregations we help to make imperfect.

Our congregations need more than money from businesspersons. They need us. They need our insights, our examples, our gifts, our participation, our love, our prayers.

Forgive my bluntness, but if you feel alienated by your congregation, forget it. We alienate people, too, even though we don't want our aggressiveness and

131

impatience to turn off people. Diversity in a congregation should be cause for joy and celebration.

I hate to think what our Christian congregations
would be like without dedicated businesspersons who
hang in and try to dispel misunderstanding and build
community.

Be a Prophet

Must all of the prophecy and proclamations come from our schools, seminaries, and institutions? Are these the only sanctuaries in which God makes his will known? Are these the only fountains of wisdom? Are these the only places at which vision is captured?

There is some good news. God is also at work in our congregations, in our pews, among our businesspersons, among our farmers, among our professional people, among our homemakers. All of us can be instruments of God to discover and reveal his will and his way. Hallelujah!

I heard someone say: "You need to go down to get to the top." Maybe we "go down" to local congregations to get to the top. Maybe at "the top" we enhance our understandings of what God wants us to be and what he wants us to do.

We need much more dialogue between our Christian institutions and our congregations. Each of us is a qualified listener and spokesperson. Theologians and businesspersons ought to be talking more with each other. We need each other to find the way.

Maybe you haven't had hands laid on you. Maybe you haven't given very many speeches. Maybe you haven't written very many articles. *But you can be a prophet,* and you need to find ways to share your visions and your insights with other brothers and sisters throughout the church.

Bankruptcy

During these postwar years of economic prosperity we have been programmed for success. Now we're facing an entirely different concern: How can a Christian fail successfully?

Economic fluctuations sometimes nudge some of our brothers and sisters into financial difficulty. And sometimes bankruptcy seems to be a way to resolve the problem.

Bankruptcy is a legal process. It uses the court system to discharge debts, satisfy creditors, and get a fresh start.

Bankruptcy is not the unpardonable sin. But it is a serious step. If used at all, it is a last resort.

Bankruptcy should never be considered a means to achieve personal gain. It does not seem Christian to borrow oneself into financial difficulty and then use bankruptcy as a way to walk away from any continuing responsibility to creditors. With or without bankruptcy, we should do everything possible to repay everything owed, if at all possible. It would be unthinkable for a Christian to maintain a high lifestyle at the expense of creditors.

During days of economic distress, our Christian congregations must be the church to persons who are experiencing financial failure.

Where Do We Go for Help?

Our businesses often prosper. But sometimes they don't. Sometimes they hit the skids and go down the tubes.

You and I know all about rough times in business. Recession. Low sales. High costs. High interest rates. Squeezed profit margins. Inadequate cash flow.

In times like those, where do we go for help? To our bankers? To our accountants? To business consultants? Sure, all of these persons may be helpful.

But what about the Christian community, the church? When do we take our business problems to church? When is it appropriate to give and receive counsel among our Christian brothers and sisters?

My point is this: As businesspersons we need the church more than ever. We need admonition, direction, encouragement, support, challenge, affirmation, confrontation.

We could be a little more open with our brothers and sisters. We could be a little more humble. We could moderate our rugged individualism a little and confess our need for community. We could acknowledge that we don't have all the answers.

Maybe small, selected groups from our congregations could be helpful. Or our pastors. Or K-groups. Or our Sunday school classes. Or the financial minis-

ters or counselors, chosen by our congregations.

Will we seek help or suffer alone? We need our Christian sisters and brothers!

Be a Happy Receiver

"It is more blessed to give than to receive" (Acts 20:35, KJV). These are the words of Jesus. Another version puts it this way: "There is more happiness in giving than in receiving."

The implication is clear. Just because there is more happiness in giving does not mean there is no happiness in receiving. Receivers are to be happy, too.

During unemployment and business distress more of us become receivers. But we don't have much experience in receiving. We don't like being on the receiving end. We don't experience much happiness when it is our business that is faltering and forcing us to require help.

Maybe we need to relax and accept the role of happy receivers, so givers can be happier.

Givers and receivers need each other. Receivers couldn't be happy if there were no givers. And givers couldn't be happy if there were no receivers.

Neither the giver nor the receiver should deprive the other of happiness.

Failing Successfully

Christian businesses are not immune to failure. In spite of our Christian faithfulness, we can get into difficulty for a variety of reasons: recession, high interest rates, low prices, overindebtedness, poor judgment, unforeseen catastrophes.

Most of us have been programmed for success. We hardly know how to handle failure. We can easily succumb to discouragement, depression, loneliness, alienation, doubt—even loss of faith in God.

Now, of course, none of us will pursue business failure just to prove how faithful we can be in failure. But when failure comes, sometimes through no fault of our own, how can we handle the failure successfully, as committed followers of Jesus?

My opinion is this: Through the pain and distress of business failure we can prosper as Christians. We can maintain our faith, our hope, our joy. We can get new perspectives on material things. We can offer positive testimonies. We can grow in humility. We can confess our continuing need for our Christian brothers and sisters.

Perhaps there are various ways to achieve spiritual success in financial failure: By rediscovering our utter dependence upon God. By thanking God for his goodness. By seeking the help we need. By praying for grace and courage to go on. By transcending any bitterness. By not allowing failure to become an obstacle to fellowship in the congregation.

It is possible to succeed even through bankruptcy. Even though bankruptcy is a last resort, success may come in various ways: By not using bankruptcy to achieve personal gain. By refusing to use the law to walk away from any continuing responsibility to creditors. By doing everything possible to repay creditors, even though bankruptcy wipes the slate clean.

Business failure can be a crucible in which we become more beautiful and more faithful Christians. But no one is saying it is a happy experience which one ought to covet.

Be Bullish

Merrill Lynch says they're bullish on America. We ought to be bullish, too. In fact, Christians ought to be the most optimistic human beings found anywhere.

Sure, our economic problems are frightening. There is no shortage of reasons for becoming pessimistic and bent out of shape: double-digit inflation, recession, high interest rates, growing indebtedness, higher taxes, declining spendable income.

We can respond to all these economic goings-on by moaning and complaining. We can get angry. We can blame big government, big business, big labor.

There's a more fitting response for Christians: We can refuse to let our economic circumstances rob us of our peace and joy. We can reinforce our trust in God. We can anchor our hope in him, and not in the present administration or the current economy. We can find new security in our community of Christian brothers and sisters.

The upward look should give us a bullish outlook.

Meditations on
MUTUAL AID

A Christian Declaration of Interdependence

Independence or interdependence? That's an appropriate question, especially in times of economic distress. When the economy goes sour, we need each other more than ever.

When things are going well, we pride ourselves in being independent. We value rugged individualism. We congratulate people who can manage their affairs all by themselves.

But how do we handle financial reverses? Why do we suffer alone? Why do we work so hard to conceal our problems? Why do we think it's a mark of weakness to seek help? Why do we simply go down the drain in painful silence?

Every July fourth Americans celebrate Independence Day, to commemorate the signing of the Declaration of Independence on July 4, 1776.

Maybe Christians should more openly express their dependence on each other, in their congregations. We need to confess our need for Christian community.

In "A Christian Declaration of Interdependence" we might say a number of things to each other:

1. Too often we let our individualism isolate us from experiencing true community with our Christian brothers and sisters.

2. Our competitive spirits sometimes get in the way

145

of trusting relationships in our congregations.

3. We feel a need to renew and demonstrate the covenant among us to "give and receive counsel."

4. We need each other more than ever in times of financial loss and disappointment.

5. We want to stand by each other in times of illness, death, accident, unemployment, and at other times of need.

6. We want to provide caring support groups for those among us who are experiencing business failure.

7. We need more openness and trust to be able to talk about our financial problems.

8. We want the unity and love of our congregational lives to exercise an inviting power on the people of our neighborhoods.

Mutual Aid Is
Good Stewardship

Two biblical concepts are inseparable: mutual aid and stewardship. You can't practice one without the other.

In stewardship we thank God for all the resources he credits to our accounts. In mutual aid we demonstrate our gratitude by using resources to help each other.

In stewardship we generously share. In mutual aid we identify some of the beneficiaries of our generosity.

In stewardship we acknowledge our accountability to God. In mutual aid this accountability becomes relevant in accountability to our brothers and sisters.

In stewardship we are nudged toward more responsible lifestyles. In mutual aid we use the liberated resources to meet the needs of others.

Mutual aid flows out of faithful stewardship. It is a demonstration of stewardship.

Mutual aid is good stewardship. And good stewardship must be expressed in mutual aid.

More Than Insurance

Christian mutual aid is more than a denominational insurance plan. Much more.

We cannot fulfill all our mutual aid responsibilities by a long-distance exchange of dollars, or according to an insurance contract. This kind of sharing is important, but at best it is "churchwide mutual aid."

Maybe we come closer to the New Testament sharing in "congregational mutual aid." In our congregations we know each other better. We are more aware of each other's hurts. We rejoice with those who rejoice and weep with those who weep. Those who have, share with those who don't have. We accept loving liability for each other.

It is in our congregations where we try to relieve the financial hardships of illness, death, loss, unemployment. A churchwide mutual aid program can undergird and supplement congregational mutual aid.

Let it be said of Christian congregations as it was said of the early church, "There is not a needy person among them." Such community would be a profound witness to the world around us.

Condominiums

I'm not against private ownership. Of course not. But I do have a question: Is there a way to avoid the extreme independence and individualism of private ownership?

Could we learn anything from condominiums? When you own a condominium you own an individual unit in a multi-unit project. There's an association of owners. Each owner has a voice and a vote in certain decisions. There's private ownership within the context of community.

This raises some interesting questions: Could we think of our private ownerships as part of a "congregational condominium"? Could we voluntarily relinquish a little bit of our individualism? Could we declare ourselves more open to the "association" of Christian brothers and sisters? Could we become more subject to the counsel of the congregation?

Each of us enjoys the freedom of choice. We can decide to proceed on our own. We can make our own independent decisions. We don't have to be accountable to anyone.

Or we can experiment with "congregational condominiums" and let some of our economic decisions be influenced by the Christian community. Wouldn't that be a happier and more secure life for all of us?

We Still Need Deacons

Years ago my grandfather was one of those deacons who was ordained for life. He collected church taxes, distributed poor funds, and administered church discipline.

Even though the job description has changed in recent years, it is my opinion that our Christian congregations need deacons more than ever. They might still be called deacons and deaconesses, or they might be known as financial ministers or financial counselors.

In our congregations we have brothers and sisters who are struggling with financial problems, which sometimes cause spiritual problems. Some persons are trying to find the way through financial success and failure, even bankruptcy. Some need help during unemployment or overindebtedness. Some ask: Which insurance policy? Which savings plan? Which retirement plan? What about budgeting?

Modern-day deacons will continue to be helpful in crisis mutual aid, when needs arise from illness, accident, or death. But there is also important work for them to do in "preventive mutual aid," to help people avoid financial crises.

These modern-day deacons would provide counsel on personal financial planning, arrange conferences

and workshops, and provide helpful materials and tools. They would be servants to fellow members who are becoming distressed and disabled over bewildering financial concerns and problems.

Mutual Aid and Evangelism

In the early church there seemed to be a strong connection between mutual aid and evangelism. According to Acts 2:44-47 (NIV), "All the believers were together and had everything in common.... They gave to anyone as he had need.... The Lord added to their number daily those who were being saved."

I have a strong conviction that our evangelistic effectiveness will be determined by the quality of our congregational lives.

In Christian mutual aid we love each other in our congregations. We care about each other. We share with each other. We help each other. We experience economic security. Who wouldn't want to become part of such a family?

A young mother accepted Christ and became a member of the congregation I pastored. I was so egotistic that I secretly hoped that my preaching helped attract her to our congregation. But that wasn't the case at all. She testified that our women loved her like she had never been loved before. She had never experienced so much help and support and encouragement.

People around us want to be part of a family. They want to experience forgiveness and love and acceptance. They want to help and be helped. They want to love and be loved. They want the security of belonging to the family of God.

Wouldn't it be surprising to discover that mutual aid may help create the kind of family circle which leads people to faith in Christ?

Self-Aid and Mutual Aid

Many of us suffer guilt when we try to justify self-aid. It seems so selfish. Mutual aid sounds more religious. We have difficulty admitting that both self-aid and mutual aid are important Christian concerns.

The Scriptures seem to offer this truth: Trying to provide for our own needs is good and proper as long as we share with others who are in need.

Jesus said, "Love your neighbor as yourself" (Matthew 19:19). The apostle Paul offered this admonition: "Make it your ambition to lead a quiet life, to mind your own business and to work with your hands, just as we told you, so that your daily life may win the respect of outsiders and so that you will not be dependent on anybody" (1 Thessalonians 4:11-12, NIV).

The Bible clearly condemns laziness and advocates work. We should provide for ourselves, as best we can, and also help others who are unable to provide for themselves.

To become preoccupied with self-aid without practicing mutual aid is to be self-centered and uncaring. To rely on mutual aid without pursuing self-aid is to be lazy and unproductive.

Both working and sharing are part of the biblical command. Both self-aid and mutual aid are part of the Christian walk.

Meditations on

COVENANTING
TOGETHER

A Covenant for Christians in Business

We proclaim our continuing desire to be faithful followers of Jesus in our everyday economic lives. We acknowledge our utter dependence upon God. We confess our need for the liberating and enabling power of God's Spirit. We covenant together, as Christian brothers and sisters called to affirm and challenge each other, to pursue greater obedience in matters related to money and economic issues.

1. We will strive to be more faithful Christian stewards of all we are and all we have.

2. We will maintain positive attitudes toward money and will attempt to use our resources according to God's will.

3. We will enjoy what God credits to our accounts and will use these possessions to further our stewardship of the gospel.

4. We will acknowledge the subtle dangers of wealth and will seek to avoid enslavement to material things.

5. We will attempt to be faithful in how we get our money as well as in what we do with it.

6. We will moderate our consumption and will attempt to adopt responsible lifestyles which demonstrate our life in Christ.

7. We will seek ways to use our money to help others rather than to embezzle God's resources for our own

selfish indulgence.

8. We will test the economic values of our society with biblical principles and corporate discernment.

9. We will continue to develop the grace of letting go and will endeavor to let New Testament standards influence our giving.

10. We will invest our material assets in ways which are in harmony with what we say we believe.

11. We will participate in congregational life and ministry, recognizing that the church needs more than our money.

12. We will not allow material success or failure to hinder the fellowship we want to enjoy in our congregations.

We pray for God's grace to become more faithful followers of Jesus Christ in our daily money and economic matters.

THE AUTHOR

John H. Rudy, Lancaster, Pennsylvania, is Eastern Regional Manager of the Mennonite Foundation. He is the former Stewardship Minister and Vice-President of Financial Services with Mennonite Mutual Aid. Since 1960 John has served with Mennonite Foundation/ Mennonite Mutual Aid, based in Goshen, Indiana.

John was a pastor and area overseer for five years in southeastern Pennsylvania. He grew up in a family business at York, Pennsylvania, then studied chemical engineering at Pennsylvania State University. Prior to 1960 he was employed for 14 years by RCA Corporation in various engineering, financial, and administrative capacities.

John is presently a director of Mennonite Economic Development Associates, Inc. (MEDA), and Menno Housing, Inc.

For Mennonite Mutual Aid John wrote *Christian Stewardship: Faith in Action*. He has published articles on stewardship, money, and economics in various

159

church papers. These meditations were first published in columns entitled "Money Matters," *Mennonite Weekly Review*, or "Auditor's Report," *The Marketplace*, published by MEDA.

John and his wife, Lucy, are the parents of three grown children. They are members of Forest Hills Mennonite Church, Leola, Pennsylvania.